Forex Trading

A Beginner's Guide to Profitable Forex Trading

By Rodney Wall

Table of Contents

Introduction 1

Chapter 1: Forex Trading - The Basics 2

Chapter 2: Online Forex Trading 7

Chapter 3: How to Trade over the Phone 12

Chapter 4: How to Time the Forex Market 13

Chapter 5: Currency Correlations 19

Chapter 6: The Seasonality of the Currency Market 24

Chapter 7: Trading Journals 27

Chapter 8: Technical Trading 46

Chapter 9: Fundamental Trading 64

Conclusion 79

Introduction

I want to thank you for downloading the book, "Forex: The Beginner's Guide to Forex Trading".

This book contains proven steps and strategies on how to succeed in the Forex market.

This eBook will teach you the fundamentals of forex trading. It will explain the different aspects of the currency market (e.g. interest rates, geopolitical issues, macroeconomic events, etc.). The insights, tactics, and strategies that you'll find in this book can help you become a skilled currency trader.

In this material, you will find clear explanations and real-world examples. You will also discover the most popular trading schemes and tactics in the currency market today. You don't have to worry if you have never read a trading/investing book before. The concepts in this book are explained using clear and understandable language.

If you are looking for a comprehensive guide to currency trading, this is the book you need.

Thanks again for downloading this book, I hope you enjoy it!

Chapter 1: Forex Trading - The Basics

This chapter explains the fundamentals of forex. It provides you with detailed information regarding currency trading and the foreign exchange market.

What is "Forex"?

Forex (also known as "FX", "foreign exchange", and "currency trading") is the largest financial market today. It also has the fastest growth rate. Each day, the forex market generates about $2.5 trillion worth of transactions. The major participants of this market are banks, traders, investors, corporations, and hedge fund companies.

How Do You Earn Money Through Forex?

The forex market is similar to the stock market: it requires the buy-low-sell-high strategy. Basically, you will purchase currencies that are low in price. Then, sell them once their price goes up.

Unlike stock purchases, however, forex transactions don't involve actual acquisitions of assets. Instead, you will deal with contracts that show the exchange rates and the amounts.

Volatility is one of the main advantages of the forex market. The value of currencies can jump multiple times. Additionally, you can multiply the daily price fluctuations through leverage.

Is it Risky?

The forex market involves various risks. If you aren't careful, forex trading can wipe out your capital (also known as "margin"). Because of this, you should never trade money that you cannot lose. Keep in mind, however, that the forex market offers unlimited profit potential.

What is a "Forex Trade"?

Forex trades are contracts that a market-maker and a trader have agreed upon. Here are the major elements of a Forex trade:

- The rate - This is the exchange rate that applies to the traded currencies. You will learn more about this later.
- The currency pair - The contract should indicate the currency you want to sell and buy.
- The nominal amount - This is the total amount of the transaction. Some traders refer to this amount as the "face" or "principal" value.

Important Note: In the forex market, your primary goal is to profit from the changes in foreign currency values. Almost all forex transactions occur because of this goal. Some individuals and organizations enter the Forex market for other reasons (e.g. to minimize business risks), but "non-profit" forex transactions are rare.

You can say that forex trades are obligations to sell and purchase specific amounts of currency pairs at predetermined rates. There is a contract, so you have to pay even if you're on the losing end of the transaction.

Extreme care is needed when trading currencies. And you cannot just make a trade after finding an attractive currency pair. You should also compare the profit potential of that investment with that of other financial instruments. For example, most forex traders compare their profit estimates with the performance of long-term U.S. bonds.

Here's a basic tactic for forex trading: buy currencies that you think will rise in value and sell the ones you think will get devalued. If your guess is correct, you can secure your profits by selling the currency back to the market.

Exchange Rates

Exchange rates are the rates at which the currency you are trading will be exchanged. Most forex transactions involve USD (i.e. the dollar of the U.S.). Some of the most popular currencies are JPY (i.e. yen), EUR (i.e. euro), CHF (i.e. franc), and GBP (i.e. pound sterling). Forex traders refer to these currencies as "the Majors".

In an exchange pair, the currency that comes first is called the "base". The second currency, on the other hand, is known as the "quote" or "counter". You can express currency pairs as fractions or ratios. Here, the counter should be the numerator while the base must be the denominator. This format specifies the amount of quote currency you need to get a unit of your base currency. Conversely, selling a unit of your base currency will give you the amount of quote currency listed on the contract.

Bears and Bulls

People who participate in the financial markets use the terms "bear" and "bull" often. Basically, these terms indicate the overall direction of the market. During a "bull market", the prices will go up. During a "bear market", on the other hand, prices will go down.

That is the reason why traders and investors acquire more assets (e.g. stocks or currencies) when the market is "bullish". If the market is "bearish", the traders and investors will likely sell off their assets.

The Different Kinds of Forex Orders

Forex brokers accept the following kinds of orders:

1. Market - This kind of order takes the prevailing market price, regardless of how high or low it is.
2. Limit - A limit order allows you to set a specific price for your transaction. Thus, the broker will have to wait until your chosen price (or prices) appear in the market.
3. Stop - A stop order is similar to a limit order: they require you to set a specific price. However, a stop order becomes a market order once your chosen currencies hit the price you set.
4. OCO - An OCO order (i.e. one-cancels-the-other order) involves two price points. One of the price points secures your profits. The other one minimizes your losses (if any).

Chapter 2: Online Forex Trading

This chapter will teach you how to trade currencies online. It will provide you with tips, tricks, and strategies that you can use to benefit from the values of foreign currencies.

How Does a Foreign Exchange System Work?

When you trade forex online, your orders will be fulfilled immediately. Exchange rates change every second. Thus, the accuracy of the quotes you see on the screen is severely limited. When you run a transaction and maybe lock in an exchange rate, the online trading system will process your request at that same moment.

Updated Exchange Rates

Because of the reason outlined above, you should use a forex computer program that shows the latest exchange rates. This kind of software continuously communicates with a server. The server, meanwhile, sends out the most updated exchange rates at any given time. Unlike the exchange rates you'll get from banks, the online data you will receive from the software is tradable. You can "lock in" (or utilize) a rate while it is on your screen.

Online Trading Platforms

Forex trading also benefits from the latest advances in technology. Many years ago, Forex traders sent their orders over the phone. This setup limited the options and potential profits of Forex traders.

Because of the modern technology, you can now trade currencies anytime you want and fund your orders using your credit card.

How to Use an Online Platform

To trade online, you should do the following:

- Sign up for an account in a trading platform
- Deposit money to fund your transactions

Trading platforms vary when it comes to their requirements and registration processes. However, the major steps are:

1. Registration - You need to do this online. Launch your favorite web browser and search for a trading platform. One you have found one, click on "Register" or "Sign up".

    a. Registration forms vary in terms of length and complexity. You have to enter personal information because governments and other authorities require it.

b. Here are the most requested pieces of information during the registration process: the name of the trader, phone number, email address, residential address, the number of a government-issued ID, and the annual income of the trader.

c. It is rare for forex platforms to conduct thorough background checks on their new members. In most cases, they assume that each user provided correct information while setting up an account.

d. *Important Note: Your chosen Forex platform will likely ask you about the source of your funds. You must declare that your funds are unquestionable. Anti-money laundering campaigns are being enforced globally, and Forex platforms are active participants. It would be best if you'll do your own research regarding money laundering before trading currencies.*

2. Fund Transfer - You should put funds in your trading account before submitting an order. Aside from the money that you'll use for your transactions, however, most trading platforms are requiring a specific amount.

This "extra money" will add more security to your trading activities. You don't have to worry since you still own the money. In fact, you might get some interest payments from the required amount.

3. Order Submission - Trading platforms are in sync with international Forex markets. Thus, the said platforms run 24 hours each day. But many platforms require their members to use specific computer programs. That means you have to use the required programs if you want to trade currencies.

4. It would be best if you'll look for a trading platform that offers browser-based access. Here, you won't have to download any program. You can also submit orders using various devices (e.g. tablets, smartphones, laptops, etc.).

Real-Time Software

Important Note: To keep things simple, this book will assume that you are using "Easy-Forex". Easy-Forex is one of the most popular platforms today. This book will give you universal information, so you don't have to worry if you are using a different platform.

Modern trading systems give up-to-date information. You won't have to refresh the page - the screen will communicate with the platform's remote server automatically.

Whenever you submit an order, the trading system will transfer the related information securely. This information will go to the platform's server, where it will be stored. Platforms guarantee data integrity by storing copies of the information in backup servers. These things happen quickly and automatically. Thus, you just have to focus on finding profitable transactions.

Chapter 3: How to Trade over the Phone

Online trading is a great option. However, you are not required to use it. If you prefer to interact with other human beings while trading currencies, you may submit your orders by phone.

Obviously, this method is more lengthy and complex than the online method. You will talk to someone else, which means you should know the proper terminologies used in forex trading. At the start of the conversation, you must indicate the information you need: do you need an "indication" or a "quote"? If you will ask for the former, you will receive general information regarding the market. You won't have to provide the currency pairs that interest you. Asking for the latter, on the other hand, requires you to give the transaction amount and the currency pairs.

It would be best if you won't specify the direction of your order immediately. Give the currency pair and wait for the dealer to say the quote. Remember that the quote is only accurate for the exact time it was retrieved. If you won't ask for an immediate execution, the quoted price will no longer be precise. Thus, you'll have to ask for another quote before placing an order.

Chapter 4: How to Time the Forex Market

As mentioned earlier, the forex market is open 24 hours each day. That means you can't monitor all of the price movements in each market. Also, you won't be able to make quick responses at all times. This is the main reason why you should follow a time-efficient trading strategy. Timing is one of the crucial factors of currency trading. Once you get it right, you'll have excellent chances of reaping profits.

This chapter will arm you with typical trading strategies. It will also give you detailed information about the volatility of currencies in relation to various time zones.

Tokyo - The Asian Session
7pm to 4am Eastern Standard Time

In Asia, forex trading occurs in regional hubs. Tokyo holds the largest share of the market, with Singapore and Hong Kong close behind. The city of Tokyo is a vital dealing hub in the Asian region, despite the issues concerning the forex market and the central bank of Japan. In fact, many forex traders base their strategies on the price momentums present in Tokyo trading sessions.

If you are risk tolerant, you should pick GBP/JPY, USD/JPY, and GBP/CHF because of their wide ranges. These currency pairs provide excellent profit potentials to short-term traders. On average, these pairs involve 90 "pips" (i.e. price interest points). Institutional investors and investment banks produce huge numbers of USP/JPY deals when entering the bond and equity markets of Japan. The central bank of Japan, which holds about $800 billion worth of U.S. securities, also affects the demand and supply of the USD/JPY pair.

If you don't like too much risk, on the other hand, you should opt for USD/CHF, GBP/USD, and AUD/JPY currency pairs. These pairs are excellent for long-term and medium-term traders who perform fundamental analysis before submitting orders. The volatility of these pairs are on a moderate level, which means you will be protected from abnormal price movements caused by speculative trades.

New York - The U.S. Session
8am to 5pm Eastern Standard Time

New York is one of the largest currency trading hubs in the world. It covers about 20% of all market turnovers each year. In addition, New York helps in stabilizing the entire currency market. Most of the trades within this session occur between 8am and 12pm. This timeframe is highly liquid because the traders in Europe are still making transactions.

If you can shoulder a lot of risks, your best choices are GBP/CHF, USD/CHF, GBP/JPY, and GBP/USD. These currency pairs offer an average daily range of 120 pips, which is excellent for day trading. Because these pairs involve the U.S. currency directly, they are more active than other options available to you.

Important Note: While the bond and equity markets of the U.S. are open, foreign investors should convert their local currency into dollar-dominated securities if they want to complete their transactions.

The U.S. currency serves as the denominator of most quotes in the forex market. In fact, currencies get exchanged for USD before undergoing any intended currency conversion (e.g. CHF to CAD). Thus, a EUR/JPY trade consists of two transactions: EUR to USD and USD to JPY. You can determine the volatility of the entire transaction based on the currency pairs' correlation.

Volatile currency pairs offer excellent profit potential. However, they also come with high risks. It would be best if you will continuously revise your trading strategy. This way, you can incorporate the volatility of currency pairs into your day-to-day tactics.

If you don't like much risk, your best options are USD/CAD, USD/JPY, and EUR/USD. The trading range of these pairs is enough to generate decent profits, but is narrow enough to curtail risks. These pairs are also liquid, which means you can minimize losses or lock in profits efficiently. The moderate volatility of these pairs is also great if you plan to hold the currencies over the long-term.

London - The European Session
2am to 12pm Eastern Standard Time

You should know that London is the most crucial trading hub right now. It holds about 30% of the entire market, which makes it the largest center in existence. The London market is highly efficient and liquid. Thus, major forex deals are often completed within the London session.

Important Note: The London market has the highest levels of volatility, due to the number of participants involved as well as the value of transactions that occur in it.

GBP/CHF and GBP/JPY are popular among risk-loving traders. On average, the daily range of these pairs exceeds 140 pips. You can put them in your portfolio if you want to generate quick cash. The volatility of these currency pairs results from the trade activities that occur in the global market.

The trading hours of London are linked to those of the Asian and U.S. sessions. Once investors and large banks have repositioned their financial portfolios, they must convert their assets into USD again as a preparation for the next U.S. session. These successive conversions are the main cause of extreme volatility of the currency pairs.

If you have a moderate level of risk tolerance, you need to acquire GBP/USD, USD/CHF, EUR/USD, and USD/CAD. These pairs have 100 pips as their average daily range. They are volatile enough to generate an acceptable level of quick returns.

For risk-averse traders, EUR/CHF, AUD/JPY, AUD/USD, and NZD/USD are great options. The daily range of these pairs is about 50 pips. With these pairs in your portfolio, you can generate profits from interests and currency trades.

When the U.S. and European Sessions Overlap
8am to 12pm Eastern Standard Time

The forex markets become highly active whenever the trading hours of Europe and the U.S. overlap. The trades during this timeframe form 70% of all forex transactions in the European market and 80% in the American market.

Important Note: If you don't want to spend your entire day in front of the computer, you should trade during this session.

When the Asian and European Sessions Overlap
2am to 4am Eastern Standard Time

This is the slowest part of any trading session. Because this overlap features thin trading, risk-loving and risk-tolerant forex traders may get some rest for two hours.

Chapter 5: Currency Correlations

As a trader, you should remember that the price changes of currency pairs are interrelated. Interest rates and economic conditions often affect multiple currencies at the same time. You can say that a relationship exists between the all the things present in the currency market. And determining the strength and overall direction of this relationship can help you earn huge profits from your forex trades. You can achieve this goal through the use of correlations.

A correlation is a calculation based on price-related information. The resulting numbers can tell you many things about the relationships present between various pairs of currencies. With this data, you can: (1) diversify your portfolio easily, (2) evaluate the risks, and (3) double your positions without acquiring the same pairs of currency.

Positive and Negative Correlations

The relationships between your currency pairs can be of great help in measuring the risks and exposure of your portfolio. For example, let's assume that you acquired many currency pairs to achieve portfolio diversification. Diversification is a useful technique when it comes to minimizing risks and losses. However, it can be counterproductive if the movements of your assets are in conflict with each other.

Correlations always appear as numbers. They highlight the similarities (or differences) of the currency pairs present in your portfolio. If the correlation value is close to 1, the connection between the currencies is strong. The strength of the connection increases as the value gets nearer to 1.

Low values indicate pairs that move opposite each other. High values, on the other hand, mark pairs that move in the same direction.

Quick Tip: Dealing with decimal values can be confusing. If you want, you can multiply the value by 100 to convert it into the percentage form.

Important Note: Correlations between currency pairs differ in terms of their strength and duration. A correlation can either be weak or strong. And it can last for a week, a month, or up to several years.

Let's assume that USD/CHF and USD/JPY have a positive correlation. These pairs move towards the same direction. Thus, acquiring both of these pairs is like investing all of your capital in a single pair. Similarly, you shouldn't acquire one of the pairs and "short" the other. That's because the results of the pairs will cancel themselves out.

Important Note: "Shorting" is a trading technique in which you'll sell an asset that you don't own. It allows you to profit from the devaluation of your chosen assets.

Negative correlations are as useful as their positive counterparts. A negative correlation exists if the correlation value of two different pairs is close to -1. This type of relationship indicates the closeness of the movements of the involved pairs. Keep in mind that negative correlations signify opposite movements.

Changing Correlations

As a forex trader, you should remember that currencies may increase or decrease in value multiple times each day. These changes in value result from the sentiment of the people and the economic conditions. Because the currencies change, the relationships between currency pairs also change. For example, the strong relationship between two currency pairs may weaken next week. You must keep your correlation values updated if you want to use them in your trading activities.

Remember: The economic conditions and market sentiments influence the relationships between currencies.

How to Calculate Correlations

Correlations change so you should know how to compute them yourself. The underlying concept might be tricky, but the computation itself is pretty straightforward. You can simplify the entire process by using a spreadsheet program (e.g. Microsoft Excel). For example, you may enter the pairs of currencies in Excel and run the correlation function.

You may choose a specific time period for this analysis. Most traders run one-month, three-month, six-month, and one-year calculations to obtain a complete view of their currency pairs. But you don't have to be this detailed. You may choose which data you'll want to study. To illustrate this concept, let's analyze the relationship between USD/CHF and USD/GBP:

- Launch Microsoft Excel.
- Obtain the pricing information for USD/CHF and USD/GBP.
- Create two columns. Label the first column CHF. The second one should be named "GBP".
- Type the pricing information in the appropriate columns (e.g. put CHF data in the "CHF" column).
- Pair the value in each column with that of USD.
- Type "=CORREL" in an empty cell.
- Highlight the entries in a column, add a comma, highlight the entries of the remaining column, and hit Enter.

- Excel will give you a number. That number is your correlation value.

Important Note: It is important to update your correlation values. However, you don't have to do it every day. Doing it twice or thrice a week is enough.

Chapter 6: The Seasonality of the Currency Market

Traders forecast the direction of currency values using technical analysis and/or fundamental analysis. Interestingly, most traders don't know that they can simplify their analysis by ignoring market indicators. You can attain this simplification through the use of seasonality.

Seasonality is a common topic among stock traders, mainly because of a phenomenon called "January Effect". In this phenomenon, the performance of stocks surge for about six days (i.e. from the final trading day of the year up to the fifth trading day of the succeeding year).

Basically, seasonality is a distinct pattern that happens at certain parts of the year. It is as noticeable in the currency market as in the stock market. Similar to stocks, currencies display excellent performance during the first few days of January. It happens because foreign investors convert their funds into the U.S. currency at the start of the year. Keep in mind, however, that currencies have different characteristics. Thus, seasonality may have greater effects on USD than on other currencies.

Currency Performance in January

Some researchers have studied the performance of currencies during the month of January. Most of their studies span ten or more years. According to these researchers, USD/CHF and EUR/USD showed the greatest effects of seasonality. These studies also show that the U.S. currency outperforms EUR 81.8% of the time.

This seasonality is also visible in the USD/CHF pair. Just like in the previous pair, USD outperformed CHF in 9 out of 11 years (or 81.8% of the time). This correlation between USD/CHF and EUR/USD is understandable because these pairs move opposite to each other.

Currency Performance During Summer

In major countries, summer reaches its peak during July and/or August. Traders are vacationing so currency values are less volatile compared to the remaining months of the year. However, it is important to note that USD/CAD and USD/JPY display a seasonality effect. Here, USD increases in value in July and falls back during August. This pattern appears 81.8% of the time.

How to Use Seasonality in Your Trades

Using seasonality in your forex trades is easy: you just have to consider it while modifying your portfolio. You don't have to do any complex analysis or evaluation. By considering the months of the year in your trading strategies, you will find lucrative opportunities you might not see otherwise.

Chapter 7: Trading Journals

This chapter will teach you how to create a trading journal. Read this material carefully: trading journals can help you become a successful forex trader.

The Importance of Trading Journals

According to experienced traders, discipline is more important than accuracy. It would be almost impossible to determine all the crucial indicators every time. But with self-discipline, you'll know the "when", "what", and "how" of your trading strategies easily.

Recording your thoughts and transactions in a journal is one of the best ways to develop self-discipline. In fact, most people in the investing world keep a journal of some sort. They use the journal to record their initial capital, entry points, and intended exit points. Often, they also list down the rationale of their investing/trading decisions. That means they can review their previous choices and make the necessary adjustments.

Important Note: Trading journals can help you learn from your mistakes and avoid unnecessary risks.

Setting Up Your Trading Journal

Creating a trading journal consists of three steps:

First Step: Generating a Currency Checklist

Your journal should begin with a printable spreadsheet. You'll fill out and print this spreadsheet on a daily basis. The checklist will help you in "understanding" the market and identifying potential trades.

Make sure that your checklist has all of the available currency pairs. Save these pairs in the leftmost column of the spreadsheet. Then, label the next three columns as "Current", "Low", and "High", respectively. Add the indicators on the right side of the file. If you want to keep things simple, you may focus on the four primary currency pairs, namely: GBP/USD, USD/CHF, EUR/USD, and USD/JPY. You may add more currencies once you gain more trading experience.

The checklist might appear to be complex and lengthy, but you should be able to fill it out in just twenty minutes. Remember that the goal of the checklist is to present the trends and trading ranges present in the currency market. Acquiring these pieces of information is a huge step towards huge profits from forex. Without a detailed idea about the market, you will blindly trade currencies. You will pick assets based on breakouts and prevailing trends. Unfortunately, this undisciplined approach often leads to huge losses.

Important Note: Market trends can give you excellent profit potential. If a pair is on an uptrend, you should buy it during retracements. If the trend is downward, however, you should sell during a rally.

The initial column of your spreadsheet's indicator group must be labeled as "ADX (14) > 25". ADX (i.e. Average Directional Index) is one of the most popular tools for evaluating trends. A trend exists if the value of the index is higher than 25. In general, high index values indicate strong trends.

The second column relies on "Bollinger bands". Strong trends usually hit one of the said bands. The third, fourth, and fifth columns, on the other hand, will hold the long-term SMAs (i.e. simple moving averages). If the numbers go below or above the averages, the market might be on a trend. You can verify the trend by checking crossovers (if any) that are in the trend's direction.

The final section of your spreadsheet should have a range group. The group's first column will contain the Average Directional Index. This time, however, you'll look for an ADX that is lower than 25. These index values indicate weak trends. The remaining columns will contain the RSI (i.e. Relative Strength

Index), traditional oscillators, and stochastic. You should conduct range trading when you have a weak ADX, high technical resistance, and oversold/overbought levels of stochastic and RSI.

Important Note: The resulting sheet can be of great help in your forex transactions. However, they are not guaranteed to work all the time. The goal of this spreadsheet is to open your eyes to the current status of the currency market.

Second Step: Identifying Potential Trades

The next part of your journal displays the trades you can make for the current trading day. Use the spreadsheet you created earlier to complete this part. Here is a basic example:

December 18, 2016
Buy USD/JPY - .8999 break (high of the previous day)
Stop at 8800 (30-day SMA).
First Target - 0.9000 (based on Fibonacci retracement)
Second Target - 0.9200 (upper Bollinger)
Third Target - Lowest point of the past ten trading days

This approach gives you clear courses of action once your desired entry price level appears. You will know the best action to take, as well as the ideal spots for your limits and stops. Keep yourself updated regarding the market conditions while working on this part of your journal.

Third Step: Listing Down the Current and/or Completed Trades

This part helps you in enforcing self-discipline. It also aids in turning your mistakes into learning opportunities. Whenever a trading day ends, take the time to review the results of your transactions. Why did you profit from a deal? What made you choose the wrong currency pair?

The main goal of this part is to determine trends and mistakes. It is likely that you are making mistakes. However, you won't know which of your actions and/or plans are faulty if you won't analyze them in detail. That means recording your transactions can help you understand your thoughts and behaviors as a forex trader. The entries in this part should look like this:

December 5, 2016

Transaction: Short 5 lots of GBP/USD @ 1.2000
Stop: 1.2500 (current all-time high)
Current Target: 1.1500

Result: The transaction got completed on the next trading day. I exited the position @ 1.300.

<u>Comments: I thought the price will drop soon, so I didn't exit at my predetermined stopping point.</u>
<u>Lesson: Stick to your trading plan.</u>

According to forex experts, an excellent trade is a trade whose fundamental and technical results match. Consequently, you shouldn't submit orders based on technical or fundamental analysis alone.

Choosing the Market Indicators

After setting up your journal, you should choose the market indicators to include in your analysis. Many forex traders fail because they consider their preferred indicators as foolproof. For example, some traders perform trades based solely on the levels of stochastic. But this strategy can result to huge losses when the currency market starts to trend. You should learn how to adapt to the changes in the market if you want to survive in the world of forex.

As a trader, you should always consider the environmental factors of the market. Prepare a list of factors so you can easily determine whether the market is range-bound or trending. Expert forex traders will tell you that selecting trade parameters plays an important role in forex.

The selection of parameters is important in every market. However, it is of the most importance in the forex market. That's because about 80% of all forex transactions are speculative. It is not surprising for currencies to stay in a specific trading environment over the long-term. In addition, the forex market is compatible with technical analysis (mainly because of the former's size).

Forex experts divide market environments into two types: trending and range trading. And defining the current market environment is the initial step of an effective trade.

Important Note: In Forex-related analyses, the shortest period of time that you can use is 24 hours. Use this timeframe even if you are making five-minute transactions.

<u>Step 1: Profiling the Environment</u>

Forex traders use various methods in determining the trading environment. There are many people who use visuals. But it would be best if you'll set specific rules in guiding your transactions. Here are some of the most popular rules today:

- Ranges

    o ADX < 20 - The ADX is an excellent indicator of a trend's strength. Indices that are lower than 20 suggest weak trends. As you probably know, weak trends often occur in range-bound markets. If the ADX is on a downtrend, the environment will likely stay in its current condition for some time.

- o Decreasing Volatility - There is a wide range of techniques that you can use in analyzing volatility. The simplest approach, however, involves comparing the short-term and long-term volatility of the market. If the short-term volatility falls after surpassing the highest point of the long-term volatility, the range trading situation is likely to reverse.

- o Volatility heightens if one or more currency pairs experience fast movements. It lowers when the trading activities are quiet and the ranges aren't wide. You can use Bollinger bands to track the volatility of the market. Narrow bands indicate small ranges and low volatility. Wide bands, on the other hand, reflect wide ranges and highly volatile trading environments.

- o Risk Reversals - Risk reversals consist of two options (i.e. a "put" option and a "call" option) on a currency. Their sensitivity and expiration are the same as that of the spot rate. Theoretically speaking, the volatility of the put and call options must be similar. But these options show different levels of volatility in the real world.

- o You can obtain crucial data through risk reversals. In fact, many traders use these reversals to evaluate existing positions.

- Trends

  - ADX > 20 - During a trending market, you should search for a rising ADX that is higher than 25. If the AFX is higher than 25 but is downward sloping, it might be a sign that the trend will disappear soon.

  - Momentum and Trend Direction - Aside from using ADX, you should also check the market's momentum indicators. Your goal is to find a momentum that matches the trend's overall direction. During an uptrend, for instance, traders will search for upward RSI, moving averages, MACD (i.e. moving average convergence/divergence), and stochastic.

    During a down trend, traders will want the said indicators to start a downward trend. If your moving averages show a perfect alignment, the momentum has considerable strength. Here are some examples of perfect alignment:

- During an uptrend - 10-day moving average > 20-day moving average > 50-day moving average, with the 100- and 200-day moving average under the short-term moving averages.

- During a downtrend - The long-term moving averages are above the short-term moving averages.

- Options - When the market is trending, you should look for reversals that favor puts or calls.

Step 2 - Identify the Time Horizon

Profiling the trading environment is not enough; you should also specify the timeframe of your intended trade. Here are some indicators and guidelines that traders use. Note that your trades don't have to meet all of the guidelines below. However, excellent trades tend to meet most of these guidelines.

- Range Trading - Intraday
    - The Rules

- Identify entry points using hourly charts.
- Confirm the existence of range trades through daily charts.
- To find entry points within a range, you may use oscillators.
- Search for RSIs or stochastic that reach extreme levels. These indicate reversals in the oscillators.
- Trades are strong when currency values maintain support levels. You have to use moving averages and the Fibonacci retracement technique for this.

- The Indicators
  - RSI
  - MACD
  - Options
  - Stochastic
  - Bollinger bands
  - Fibonacci retracement

- Range Trading - Medium-Term

  - The Rules

    - Focus on daily charts.
    - You have two choices:

- Look for upcoming opportunities - Search for volatile markets, where long-term volatility levels are considerably lower than short-term ones.
- Play in current ranges - Identify active ranges using Bollinger bands.
- Search for one or more reversals in the market oscillators (e.g. stochastic).
- Check the price action - the price should fall at important resistance points and rise on important support points. You can use the traditional indicators for this task.
- Make sure that the ADX is lower than 25. A falling ADX is great, but not mandatory.

- The Indicators

  - RSI
  - MACD
  - Options
  - Stochastic
  - Bollinger bands
  - Fibonacci retracement

- Trend Trading - Medium-Term

  - The Rules

- Find trends using daily charts. Check weekly charts to prove the existence of trends.
- Analyze the market's characteristics. What parameters are satisfied?
- Go for retracement/breakout situations on moving averages or Fibonacci levels.
- The trade shouldn't have any significant resistance levels in front of it.
- Check your trade using candlestick patterns.
- Enter the market during significant lows or highs.
- It would be best if you'll wait for the contraction of volatilities before entering the market.
- The fundamental characteristics of the currency pairs (e.g. growth) should be positive.

- The Indicators

  - RSI
  - Elliott waves
  - Fibonacci retracement
  - ADX
  - Parabolic SAR (i.e. Stop and Reversal)
  - Ichimoku Clouds

- Breakout Trading - Medium-Term

    o The Rules

        - Concentrate on daily charts.
        - Search for contractions in the short-term volatility levels. The contraction point should be way much lower than the long-term volatility levels.
        - Confirm breaks using pivot points.
        - The moving averages should favor the trade.

    o The Indicators

        - Fibonacci Levels
        - Moving Averages
        - Bollinger Bands

Managing Risks

The concept of risk management is easy to understand. However, many traders fail to consider it when choosing, buying, holding, and selling currencies. There are countless situations where profitable positions became losing ones, and excellent strategies became horrible financial blunders. Your IQ and your knowledge about the market don't guarantee success in the forex market. If you pay little attention to risk management, your trades will likely lead to losses.

In a nutshell, risk management consists of defining the risks you can shoulder and the profits you want to get. Without these pieces of information, chances are you will exit the market prematurely or remain in losing market positions. It is not uncommon for forex traders to have more profitable positions than losing ones, but end up with huge losses instead of profits.

The following guidelines will help you in managing risks:

- Stop-Loss Orders - These orders assist you in specifying maximum losses. By setting a stop-loss order, you can prevent horrible positions from ruining the profitability of your entire portfolio. A trailing stop is particularly useful in securing your earnings. Successful traders usually adjust their stops whenever their assets increase in value. Meanwhile, some traders close a segment of their existing positions.

    o Treat new transactions as if they are independent ones, regardless of whether your positions are winning or not. This approach is excellent if you want to ride a trend or gain more profitable positions. When adding to an existing position, analyze the currency as if it is not in your portfolio yet. If the favorable trend continues, you may close a segment of your position while adjusting your stops. This task requires you to consider the rewards you want to get and the risks you can shoulder.

- How to Use Stop-Loss Orders - Because money management is important in successful forex trading, you should always implement stop-loss orders in your positions. Keep in mind that these orders specify the highest amount of loss that you'll experience. If the value of the currency hits your stopping point, your position will close quickly and automatically. Thus, utilizing stop-loss orders can greatly reduce the risks involved in your trades.

- Placing a Stop-Loss Order on Your Trades - Traders implement stop-loss orders in two ways:

    o Parabolic SAR - You'll find this indicator in most forex charting computer programs. In a nutshell, Parabolic SAR shows the best position for the stop-loss order as a dot.

    o Two-Day Low Approach - With this approach, you will place the order 10 pips lower than the pair's two-day low. For instance, if the pair's current value is 1.1300 and its two-day low was 1.1280, you should place the stop at 1.1270.

- Risk-Reward Ratios - You must specify the risk-reward ratio of all your trades. Basically, this ratio states that amount you can lose, and the amount you want to earn. Your ratios should be 1:2 or better. Setting these ratios before entering the market can help you avoid financial losses.

The Psychological Aspects of Currency Trading

Choosing the right indicators and monitoring the trading environment can certainly help you in your trading adventures. However, you cannot underestimate the effects of your psychological outlook on your trades. By having the appropriate psychological outlook, you can boost your chances of succeeding in the forex market.

Controlling Your Emotions

Do not allow your emotions to affect your trading decisions. The most successful traders display emotional detachment: they don't build emotional connections with the assets they acquire. They consider objectivity as an important part of their toolbox. Unskilled traders, on the other hand, make huge mistakes because they base their trades on their emotions. They switch to another plan after experiencing some losses, or become reckless after getting some profits.

Taking a Break

If you are experiencing consecutive losses, you should avoid trading to stop greed and/or fear from influencing your decisions.

You will face unprofitable transactions over the course of your trading career. Thus, you should be prepared to cope with financial losses. Traders, even the best ones, experience losing streaks. To succeed, however, you should display tenacity and concentration while going through such rough times.

Stop trading when you are on a losing streak. In most cases, forgetting about the market for several days is an effective solution to your dilemma. Sticking to your trading routine in an unfavorable market condition can lead to huge losses. And these losses can destroy your self-confidence and psychological condition. Accept your mistakes. It would be impossible to profit from all of your transactions. You will make mistakes; and your ultimate goal is to keep the damaging effects of your errors at a manageable level.

Here are some rules that you should remember:

- Do not go against the trend.
- Determine the expectations in the market.
- Define the risk-reward ratio of your trades.
- Allow your returns to increase.
- Minimize your losses.
- Secure sufficient capital.
- If you have a losing position, don't add to it.
- Record your thoughts and actions using a journal.
- Assign maximum losses or profit retracements.
- Make sure that your positions have logical sizes.

Chapter 8: Technical Trading

This chapter will focus on the technical aspects of currency trading. It will give you detailed information about the technical strategies that successful forex traders use.

Multiple Timeframe Evaluation

You should be selective if you want to be successful in intraday trading. Most hedge funds rely on trend trading. Many traders choose range trading over trend trading, but huge profits often result from prolonged movements of the market. Mark Boucher, an expert money manager, stated that 70% of the movements have 20% chance of occurring at any given time. That means performing multiple timeframe analyses can help you maintain your view of the market's overall status.

Important Note: In the forex market, selling during a downtrend or buying during an uptrend is much better than picking tops and/or bottoms.

Most traders conduct multiple timeframe analysis using different types of charts. They determine the trend through daily charts. And they identify entry levels using hourly charts. To illustrate this method, let's analyze the historical performance of the AUD/USD currency pair.

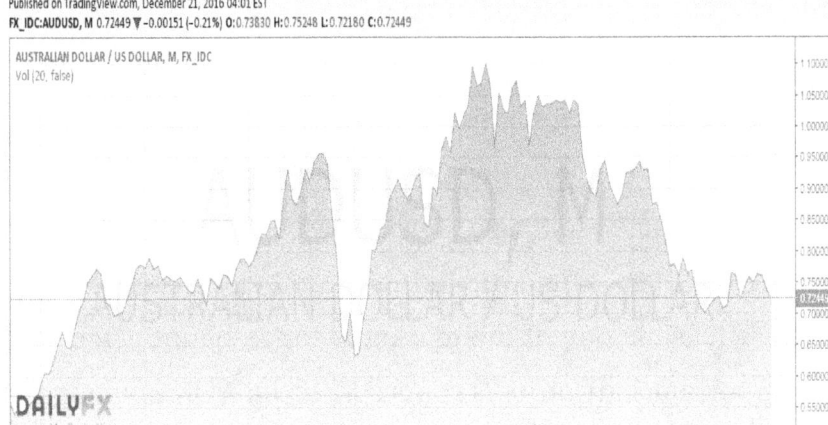

Source: www.dailyfx.com

As you can see, the pair trended high during the 2009-2011 period. This period surely gave range traders a difficult time, since the pair established new record highs. The top pickers who went for this currency pair might have lost large sums of money.

In that kind of period, it is best if you'll enter the market and ride the trend. This scheme requires traders to make purchases during temporary price reductions. The www.dailyfx.com website allows you to adjust the timeframe of your charts. You can just switch it to "daily" and "hourly" charts to get the information you need. For instance, you may analyze the trend through daily charts and find the ideal entry points using hourly charts.

The multiple timeframe evaluation technique is an important tool. In fact, you cannot overestimate its importance regardless of the current market environment. Thinking about the overall trend will help you avoid bad trades. Most inexperienced traders focus on range trading because selling during highs and buying during lows is a simple concept. This strategy works, of course, but forex traders should also consider the environment they are planning to enter. As mentioned in the previous chapter, range trading is feasible only if the market is range-bound. One of the most important indicators is the ADX. If the ADX is lower than 25 and is downward sloping, the market is conducive to range trading.

Double Zeros

Market structure is an aspect of trading that can lead to excellent profits. Unfortunately, many traders ignore or underestimate it. Thus, gaining a deep knowledge of market dynamics and structure can give you a significant advantage. With this kind of knowledge, you will be able to execute tactics for exploiting intraday price fluctuations.

You should know the dynamics of the market if you want to be a successful forex trader. That's because order flow plays an important role in intraday price changes. Independent traders rarely have access to sell-side order flow information. To benefit from short-term price adjustments, you must know how to anticipate the ideal price zones. This is one of the best techniques for day trading since you won't be "playing" against your market maker.

In intraday trading, you can't get large profits just by trading on the faults of all resistance or support levels. Success requires being selective: don't enter the market unless a favorable reaction is likely. You can identify these opportunities by taking advantage of psychologically important trading levels (e.g. round numbers, double zeros, etc.).

Basically, double zeros are numbers whose last pair of digits are both zeros (e.g. 104.00, 99.00, 123.00, etc.). You should count how many times the currency pair will hit double zero resistance or support levels, regardless of the overall trend. Here, you will find that the price fluctuations are greater than those present in other areas. Intraday traders can greatly benefit from this kind of reaction because the potential rewards can go up to 50 pips. The risks, on the other hand, are about 20 pips and below.

This technique is easy to execute. But it requires you to understand the market and the mentality of other market participants. This technique works because it has a logical basis. Huge banks with order flow access have better positions than other players in the market. The order books of these participants give them firsthand information regarding the possible reactions at various levels of prices. Often, dealers use this data to set their own short-term positions.

In general, market participants place conditional orders in nearby levels. Although a stop-loss order is usually found past round numbers, forex traders will set their take-profit (also known as T/P) orders on the round number. This tendency results from the fact that humans use round numbers when thinking. Consequently, T/P orders are often located at double zero levels. The forex market is continuous, so limit and stop orders are more common here than in the stock market.

Huge banks that can access order flows, such as limits and stops, try to exploit the aforementioned clusters to gun stops.

Important Note: To gain more profits from this technique, you should verify the importance of double zeros using other market indicators.

<u>The Rules of the Strategy</u>

Short

- Find currency pairs that trade higher than their intraday 20-period SMA on 10-minute charts.
- Short the pairs at 10 (or lower) pips under than the current figure.
- Set a protective stop at 20 pips under your entry price point.

- If the profitability outweighs the risks, close 50% of your position. Then adjust the protective stop to reach a break-even point. Move the stop up if the price changes are in your favor.

Long

- Find a pair that trades below the intraday 20-period SMA. You may use a 10-minute or 15-minute chart for this.
- Buy the pair at 10 pips (or lower) above the current value.
- Place a protective stop on the pair. Make sure that your entry price is higher than the stop by 15 to 20 pips.
- If the trade proves to be profitable, close 50% of your position and adjust your stop. Change the placement of your stop if the price fluctuations are in your favor.

Market Conditions

You'll get the most benefits from this strategy if the price movements aren't caused by economic factors. Simply put, the strategy becomes highly effective if the trading environment is quiet. Traders use this strategy when currency pairs have tight trading ranges.

Optimizing the Strategy

Round number price levels become stronger if they jibe with a major technical level. That means the strategy becomes more reliable if other resistance or support levels intersect.

Waiting for Real Numbers

In the forex market, volume information is not available to day traders. That is the main reason why day traders don't rely on demand levels. Rather, these people make trades based on the market's micro structure. The most exploited aspect of the market is its 24-hour nature. People can make trades around the clock, but the activities within the trading sessions vary.

As mentioned in an earlier chapter, the Asian session is the most "silent" session in the world of forex. This session generates the tightest ranges for the GBP/USD and EUR/USD pairs. Recent surveys have shown that the U.K. session is the most active: it forms 31% of all forex transactions. If you'll add the numbers from France, Switzerland, and Germany, the European market holds 42% of all currency trades. The U.S., which holds 19% of all transactions, comes second at the "most active list".

The information given above highlights the importance of the U.K. session. Trading in the London market lets you exploit the news and/or events that occurred during the overnight Tokyo session or the final part of the New York session.

GBP becomes active against USD during the London and European trading sessions. Active trades also occur during the European/Unites States overlap, but aside from the said sessions, the currency pair gets traded lightly. This decrease in intensity occurs because most GBP/USD trades occur through the market makers in Europe. Basically, day traders can obtain the earliest intraday moves. These moves typically occur at the start of the U.K. session.

The strategy outlined above works because traders in the U.K. market are known for hunting stops. That means the first few movements in the London session may be untrue. The European and British dealers serve as the main market makers of the GBP/USD pair, so they have a lot of information regarding the pair's actual demand and supply. This strategy begins when interbank desks check their books and utilize the data of their clients to gain pip differentials by initiating close stops. After taking the stops out and clearing the books, the true move of the GBP/USD pair will start. When that occurs, you may use the strategic rules given below.

Important Note: Economic releases and the opening of the U.S. session improve the effectiveness of this strategy. Here, you'll trade the currency pair once the noise dies down.

The Rules of the Strategy

Short

- The GBP/USD pair opens in the European market. It trades 25 pips higher than the top points of the London and Frankfurt sessions.
- The currency pair depletes its gains.
- Place an order that sells the pair at 10 pips under the ranges low.
- Set a stop-loss order about 20 pips from the entry price.
- If the slowness of the position outweighs the risks, cover half of it and trail your stop order.

Long

- Wait for the currency pair to set a new low. The low should be 25 pips higher than the initial price.
- The pair will reverse its course.
- Set an order that buys the currency at 10 pips higher than the range's top point.
- Make sure that you have a stop-loss order for the pair. The distance of this stop from your entry point cannot exceed 20 pips.
- Cover half of your position if its slowness outweighs the risks. Put a trailing stop-loss order on your remaining position.

Inside Day Play

Professional traders consider volatility trading as one of their best tools. These traders interpret the changes in volatility levels using various methods. But the simplest option involves representing the volatility levels visually. Experts have been using this method for a long time, but inexperienced traders are still surprised by its reliability, simplicity, and accuracy. Through candle charts, you can determine inside days quickly and easily.

The term "inside day" refers to a day whose low and high are less than those of the previous trading day. For example, today's low and high shouldn't exceed yesterday's low and high. Volatility play requires two or more consecutive inside days. The chances of an upward volatility surge increase with the number of inside days that will occur. Experts execute this strategy using daily charts, but longer timeframes offer better breakout opportunities.

There are traders who use hourly charts for the inside day strategy. However, the short timeframe decreases the chances of success. It would be best if you'll use daily charts while trading.

If you prefer hourly charts, you should wait for a contraction to occur before the opening of the U.S. or London market. Your goal is to anticipate a real breakout while avoiding false ones.

Using daily charts, on the other hand, lets you find breakouts for specific currency pairs before economic releases. You can use this strategy on any currency pair, but false breakouts are unlikely to occur in pairs with tight ranges (e.g. EUR/CHF, AUD/CAD, USD/CAD, EUR/CAD, etc.).

The Rules of the Strategy

Short

- Look for a pair with consecutive inside days. A trading day is an inside day if its low and high don't exceed those of the previous trading day.
- Sell the pair 10 pips under the latest inside day's low.
- Identify the latest inside day's high. Use that value as the basis for your stop order.
- Reap your profits when the prices greatly outweigh the money you risked. Alternatively, you may trail your stop order.

Long

- Find a pair with at least two consecutive inside days.
- Enter a long position 10 pips higher than the latest inside day's high.
- Set a stop order for a pair of lots 10 pips under the latest inside day's low.

- Get your profits once the prices greatly exceed your capital. Trailing the stop is a great alternative.

Optimizing the Strategy

To boost the effectiveness of this strategy, you may use technical patterns with your visual identifiers. This method will help you learn more about the breakout's direction. For instance, if the pair's inside days build and contract to the apex of a range, an upside breakout is likely to occur. The reversed version of this method also works: a downward breakout is likely if the pair's inside days contract and build towards the floor of a range. The technical factors that you can use include resistance levels, support levels, and triangle formations.

Important Note: This strategy becomes riskier if you are using daily charts. But the payout is also great. You can trade aggressively by acquiring two or more positions. This approach will help you secure profits from the first 50% of your position when the prices exceed your capital. Use trailing stops on the rest of your position. In general, breakout trades come before huge trends. That means trailing stops will allow you to reap some profits while riding the market trend.

The Fader

In many cases, traders position themselves for potential breakouts, but end up with range-bound price movements. You should also remember that significant breakouts don't guarantee success: you need continuous breakouts to get your desired profits. If the breakout reaches a notable level, traders and/or interbank dealers will attempt to push the prices past the current breakout level for a bit. Each breakout level is important, so there are no specific rules when it comes to sustaining trends.

Trading in breakout levels involves huge risks. Because of this, false breakouts are more common than real ones. There are situations where the market prices challenge resistance levels several times before going on a breakout. The said situations led to the birth of contra-trend forex traders, people who earn money by fading breakouts. But fading all breakouts can be too risky, since real breakouts might occur. As you probably know, real breakouts have considerable strength and duration.

When fading breakouts, you should have a set of rules for filtering price patterns. This kind of criteria will help you identify the realness of breakouts. The rules you'll find below can serve as the foundation of your own criteria.

Important Note: This strategy is similar to the strategy called "Waiting for Real Numbers". You will identify range-bound environments using daily charts. To determine entry levels, you have to use hourly charts.

<u>The Rules of the Strategy</u>

Short

- Identify a pair whose ADX for the past 14 days is lower than 35.
- Wait until the market surpasses the high of the previous trading day by about 15 pips.
- Enter a short position at 15 pips under the low of the previous trading day.
- Set an initial stop once your order gets filled. Make sure that the stop is 30 pips higher than your entry price.
- Get your profits once the pair doubles the capital you risked.

Long

- Find a pair whose ADX for the past 14 days is lower than 35. It would be great if the ADX is on a downward trend: this signals the further weakening of the trend.

- Monitor the pair. Once the market price becomes lower than the low of the previous trading day by 15 pips (or higher), proceed to the next step.
- Buy the currency pair 15 pips greater than the high of the previous trading day.
- Once your order is filled, set a stop order 30 pips from your entry price.
- Get your profits once the price of the currency pair outweighs the risks by at least 60 pips.

Optimizing the Strategy

The effectiveness of this strategy decreases if there is a scheduled release of important economic information. This kind of information can initiate unexpected price movements in the financial markets. This strategy is your best bet if the currency pair has low volatility levels and narrow trading ranges.

Screening Fake Breakouts

Breakout trading can be highly profitable. But it comes with considerable risks since breakouts tend to fail, especially in the forex market. This tendency results from the fact that forex is technically driven. Consequently, there are countless market players who deliberately break pairs to absorb other traders.

You can screen price actions to identify the realness of breakouts. The rules you'll find below are designed to exploit trending markets. The trending markets involved here reach new highs, take recent lows, and move up again to record other highs. With this approach, you will be able to enter a trending market once the weak participants are gone. Here, the significant players will rejoin the market to boost the pair's ascent.

The Rules of the Strategy

Short

- Search for a pair with a potential 20-day low; monitor it.
- Wait for the currency pair to go through a reversal. It should hit a two-day high in a three-day timeframe.
- Put a sell order once the pair trades under its 20-day low.
- Wait for the currency pair to rise several ticks above the previous two-day high.
- Take your profits once the pair doubles the money you risked. If you want, you may use trailing stops to keep your funds in the market.

Long

- Find a pair with a potential 20-day high and monitor it.

- Wait for the currency pair to experience a reversal. Specifically, the pair should hit a two-day low in a period of three days.
- Purchase the currency pair once it gets the aforementioned high.
- Set a stop order several pips under the low you found in the second step.
- Take your profits once the pair doubles the amount you risked. As an alternative, you may keep your funds in the market and protect your gains by trailing stops.

The Channel Strategy

This strategy works well in the forex market. That is because currencies tend to build lasting trends: narrow trading ranges are rare in forex. By perusing several charts, you will see that channels frequently occur and that you can identify them easily. It is not unusual for independent market participants to conduct channel trading within the Asian hours and breakout trading in the U.S. or London session. Also, there are many cases where the release of economic data initiates channel breaks. That means you should always consider economic releases while trading currencies.

If there is an existing channel, the U.S. is about to release a huge number, and a pair is at the channel's apex, a breakout is likely to occur. This scenario requires buying, not short-selling.

You can create a channel by plotting a trend and drawing a line parallel to it. The price fluctuations of the currency pair must appear between the channel lines. Your goal is to determine the periods where the pair trades inside a slender channel, and trade towards a breakout. This strategy becomes highly effective if used before an important market event.

To make long trades with this technique, you should:

- Find a channel using a daily or intraday chart. The range of the price movements should be narrow.
- Enter a long position in case the pair exceeds the channel's upper line.
- Set a stop order right under the same line.
- Adjust the stop order according to the price changes.

Chapter 9: Fundamental Trading

Technical strategies are not enough. You should also include some fundamental trading strategies in your toolbox if you want to succeed. In this chapter, you'll learn the basics of fundamental trading. You will also discover the fundamental trading strategies that expert forex traders use.

Choosing the Best Currency Pairs

Many traders judge pairs based on the characteristics of one of the currencies. But this is a huge mistake. You are dealing with a currency pair, so the value of the trade depends on both of the currencies involved. In the forex market, neglecting economic conditions can reduce the profits you can get. It can also increase the chances of financial losses. If your trade is against a stout economy, the chances of failing is high: your preferred currency might plummet in value, leaving you defenseless against a strong currency. In a similar manner, there is a possibility that the second currency might get stronger, giving you microscopic gains. Thus, you should identify good economic pairings if you want to maximize profits.

In March 2005, for instance, Federal Reserve of the U.S. increased its inflation risks through the FOMC (Federal Open Market Committee) statement. This event led to the dominance of the U.S. dollar against other currencies. The strength of the

American currency further improved because of positive economic data from the said country. You could have profited from any long USD position during that time, but the appreciation of the U.S. dollar was more powerful and stable against certain currencies. For instance, when the first bloodbath had passed, the British pound rose while the Japanese yen plummeted. The rise of the British currency occurred because the economy of Great Britain experienced impressive growth.

The continuous fall of the Japanese currency, meanwhile, occurred because market participants doubted the capability of Japan's economy. During that time, Japan showed signs of recession and didn't have any economic expansion. Thus, the strength of USD had more impact against JPY than GBP because of economic reasons.

Geopolitical events can have considerable impact on the forex market. When analyzing equal trades, however, pairing a strong economy against a weak economy can give you better chances of success.

The Leveraged Carry Strategy

This strategy is a favorite of investment banks and hedge fund companies. Traders refer to this strategy as the "classic international macro trade". Basically, this strategy involves entering long market positions. People who use this strategy also short/sell low-yield currencies and purchase high-yield ones.

Aggressive traders won't hedge against their exposure to exchange rates. Thus, speculators expect high-yield currencies to increase in value while interest rate differentials generate income. For people who hedge the exposure to exchange rates, the interest rates can generate substantial returns. This is easy to understand: a 3% differential can turn into 30% if you will have 10x leverage. Keep in mind that leverage can lead to losses if used recklessly. The appreciation of capital happens when many traders find an opportunity and put their money in it. This tendency helps currency pairs in starting upward rallies.

The law of demand and supply influence the financial markets. Because of this economic principle, funds enter and exit various markets. Countries and markets that provide high investment returns attract most of the available capital. Thus, high interests lead to an increase in demand for any currency. You can utilize this information through the leveraged carry strategy.

If you will implement "leveraged Carry" properly, you can minimize risks and generate huge returns. Keep in mind, however, that each trade comes with some risks. You will likely lose your hard-earned money if you don't know the "when", "why", and "how" of carry trading.

How Does a Carry Trade Work?

You can implement this strategy by purchasing currencies that offer high interest rates and selling currencies with low interest rates. It has a high level of profitability because it exploits interest rate differentials between different currencies. Here's a basic example:

The interest rate of the U.S. dollar is 4.5% while that of the British pound is 1%. You can execute a carry trade by buying USD and selling GBP. By doing so, you can reap 3.5% of your capital as profits (4.5% minus 1%) if there will be no changes in the currencies' exchange rates. The 3.5% profit is computed without any leverage. With 5x leverage, you can get about 17.5% of your capital as profits. Note that this computation focuses on interest-related returns only.

Important Note: It is likely that other market participants will discover this trading opportunity. When that happens, your chosen currency pair will undergo value appreciation. That means you will have two sources of profits: capital appreciation and interest rate differential.

Why Does it Work?

A carry trade works due to the continuous movement of funds between different countries. Countries usually attract investors using high interest rates. If a nation has a good economy (e.g. high productivity, rising incomes, high growth, etc.), it can offer high ROI (i.e. return on investment) to foreign investors. In other words, countries with attractive growth potential can pay higher rates of interest to investors.

Investors love high interest rates. They look for investment opportunities that provide great rates of return. Before making an investment, investors typically choose those options that offer the best ROI. If many investors will use this approach, large volumes of capital will enter countries with high levels of return.

Countries with subpar economic performance, on the other hand, cannot offer high return rates. Actually, there are some countries that cannot provide any ROI because of their poor economy.

The difference between the interest rates of various countries fuel the "Carry Trade Strategy". At this point, let's add more details to the example given above:

A person has a bank account in Britain. This account gives an annual interest rate of 1%. Meanwhile, a bank in the U.S. offers an annual interest rate of 4.5%. The difference in interest rates attracts the investor: he wants to earn more money through his capital.

Let's say the investor found a way to convert his British pounds (with 1% interest rate) to U.S. dollars (with 4.5% interest rate). In this situation, you can say that the investor "sold" his British pound deposit to "buy" a U.S. dollar deposit. When the requisite processes are completed, the investor will have a U.S. bank account that gives 3.5% more interest than his previous bank.

If a huge number of people will do the "buy and sell" activity described above, capital will flow from Great Britain to the U.S. That's because investors will trade their British pounds for American dollars. The U.S. attracts more capital thanks to its high interest rates. The flow of capital into the U.S. bolsters the market value of its currency.

How to Time Carry Trades

The effectiveness of this strategy varies depending on how you time it. Actually, you can get the most out of carry trading when market participants have a common attitude regarding risks.

Does it Involve a lot of Risks?

The moods of market participants have a tendency to change as time goes by. Traders can be risk-lovers today and risk-averse next week. This tendency is still evident if you'll consider all market participants as a single unit.

When forex traders show a collective willingness to shoulder risks, they are in a "risk-seeking mood". On the contrary, traders who display conservativeness are said to be in a "risk-fearing mood". The concept of risk aversion is important here. When the market has low levels of risk aversion, the participants are more daring than usual. If risk aversion is at high levels, however, the participants simply want to protect their assets.

The profitability of carry trading increases when risk aversion is low. This fact is easy to understand if you'll think about the activities involved in carry trading. As mentioned earlier, carry trades involve selling low-interest currencies and purchasing high-interest currencies. And buying high-interest currencies is risky: you can't be sure whether the strong economy will continue to perform positively. Regardless of how strong a national economy looks, there's still a possibility that something will happen to ruin it all. As an investor, that is one of the major risks you'll have to face.

If investors are unwilling to shoulder this risk, money won't flow between different countries and you won't be able to execute carry trading. Simply put, the carry trading strategy can only be used in markets that have low levels of risk aversion.

When is it Ineffective?

A carry trade is ineffective when the market has high levels of risk-aversion. Investors are not willing to gamble their investments. Consequently, they wouldn't want to invest in risky currencies regardless of the interest rates involved. When investors are risk-averse, they prefer to stash away their funds in low-interest, risk-free assets. Basically, these people are selling high-interest currencies to purchase low-interest ones.

More Information About Risk Aversion

The profitability and effectiveness of carry trading depend on the risk aversion of the traders. Thus, you should always gauge the levels of risk aversion in the market before executing the carry trading strategy. In addition, you must monitor every change in the market's risk aversion levels.

An increase in risk-aversion is great for low-interest currencies. In many cases, the moods of investors change quickly. These "mood swings" occur because of major events in the world. When risk aversion gets a quick upsurge, the available capital goes into low-interest, risk-free financial vehicles.

Measuring the levels of risk-aversion is not easy. There is no surefire way to get the needed results. However, one of the simplest ways to get an idea about risk-aversion levels is by checking the yields offered by bonds. Bonds differ in terms of their credit ratings - if the spread (i.e. the difference) between these bonds is wide, the risk-aversion level of investors is high. You can get bond-related information online or from financial newspapers.

Other Factors to Consider

Risk aversion plays an important role in carry trading. But it is not the only factor that traders should consider. The list given below will give you three things to think about when contemplating a carry trade:

- Appreciation of low-interest currencies - Your profits (if any) will result from the difference between the interest rates of your chosen currencies. The wider the gap, the bigger the profits. However, you will lose your money if the low-interest currency experiences an increase in value.

- Risk aversion is not the only market element that affects currency value. For example, significant improvements in the economic condition of a country will result to the appreciation of its currency. That means you should always check the economic attributes of a currency before trading it.

- Trade balances between nations - Trade balances (i.e. the import-export differential) can also influence the effectiveness of your carry trades. You've learned that low risk-aversion levels lead to the transfer of capital from low-interest currencies to high-interest currencies. This is a natural reaction, but it doesn't happen all the time.

To illustrate this concept, let's analyze the import-export situation in the U.S. The U.S. has low return rates, but risk-averse traders still want to put their capital there. Why does it happen? It's simple: the U.S. has a tremendous trade deficit (i.e. the exported goods are less than the imported goods). And this deficit requires the funding of foreign countries. This trade deficit pulls continuous capital from foreign investors, regardless of the ROI.

- Time horizon - The carry trading strategy is designed for long timeframes. Before using this strategy, make sure that you can hold the position for six months or more. You should be committed to the strategy; otherwise, the temporary price fluctuations might distract you or force you to exit the market prematurely. It is also important control your leverage. Too much leverage can stop you from maintaining your positions.

Monitoring Macroeconomic Events

Inexperienced traders concentrate on the economic events of the current week: what happened and what would be the effects on their short-term positions. This approach is enough for some people, but you should also consider huge events that can affect the economy. That's because huge macroeconomic events often cause considerable changes in the financial markets. No, the changes involved here are not limited to temporary price setbacks. Depending on the scope and size of the macroeconomic event/s, the perception towards one or more currencies can change drastically.

Major events (e.g. wars, natural disasters, international meetings, etc.) wield widespread effects in the forex market because of their irregularity. These events trigger different reactions in the market: some currencies will soar while others will plummet. Thus, monitoring global events, forecasting the overall direction of the market sentiment, and preparing accordingly can lead to amazing profits.

Here are some events to consider:

- Presidential elections
- Meetings between central banks
- Possible changes in currency regimes
- Important meetings between G7/G8 finance ministers.

- Possible wars resulting from geopolitical conflicts
- Major summits

The Price of Commodities

Commodities (e.g. oil, gold, etc.) are linked to the currency market. Knowing the effects of commodities on currencies can help you evaluate risks, anticipate price adjustments, and comprehend overall exposure. Thinking about commodities while trading Forex might seem strange at first, but the movements of commodity prices are similar to that of currencies.

As mentioned earlier, the four primary currencies are considered as commodities. These currencies are: CHF (Swiss franc), CAD (Canadian dollar), NZD (New Zealand dollar), and AUD (Australian dollar). All of these currencies have strong relationships with the price of gold. In the said countries, currency laws and gold reserves lead to almost identical price movements. The Canadian currency has a tendency to move parallel to oil prices, but this relationship is weak and complex.

Important Note: Correlation differs from one currency to another. This is the main reason why price changes in the commodity market reflect the changes in the currency market, and vice versa. Understanding price movements, knowing their direction, and determining the performance of the corresponding asset can assist you in discovering profitable trends.

The Connection

Oil

The price of oil has a tremendous effect on the global economy. Thus, the relationship between this commodity and the prices of currencies is complex and unstable. Actually, only the Canadian currency shows some similarities with the price of oil.

The correlation value between oil and USD/CAD is 0.4. This weak number indicates that increases in the price of oil don't guarantee value appreciation for the Canadian currency. Canada is one of the world's major oil producers, but the country doesn't get substantial economic benefits from changes in oil prices.

Canadians demand a lot of oil products because of their country's cold climate. In addition, Canada is highly vulnerable to changes in economic conditions since it relies on exports heavily.

Gold

Prior to discussing the connection between gold and the Forex market, let's talk about the relationship between the U.S.

currency and gold. Despite the fact that the U.S. is one of the largest gold producers in the world, increases in the price of gold don't lead to the appreciation of USD. In fact, when gold increases in value, the American dollar gets devalued. The opposite is also true: gold loses its value when the American dollar gets a price increase. This strange event happens because of the investors' perception about gold. When geopolitical conflicts arise, investors relinquish their USD positions and put their funds in gold. Some investors even use the term "ant dollar" when referring to this precious metal. To sum it all up, the price of gold goes up when USD falls because investors leave the currency market for the safety that gold offers.

The AUD/USD pair has excellent positive correlation with gold. It's correlation value is 0.80. That means the value of AUD goes up when the value of gold increases. The performance of the NZD/USD pair is similar to the previous one, mainly because the economy of New Zealand is closely related to that of Australia. The Canadian dollar has a stronger relationship with gold. The correlation between these two is at 0.84. CHF has the highest correlation with gold. It's correlation value is 0.88.

Important Note: If the price of gold is on an upward trend, you may get a long position on any of the commodity currencies mentioned in this book.

Using the Information in Your Trades

Knowledge about commodity prices can help you in two ways. First, you can utilize the data as leading indicators for upcoming changes in the price of currencies. It is not uncommon for forex traders to predict price changes based on the performance of oil and/or gold.

As an alternative, you may trade other assets to exploit your knowledge regarding commodities. This approach helps you in injecting some diversification into your trading portfolio. For example, if you think that the value of oil and/or gold will increase, you may acquire the corresponding currency pair/s. A distinct advantage offered by currency trading over purchasing commodity futures is that the former allows you to earn profits through interest rate differentials.

Conclusion

Thank you again for buying and downloading this book!

I hope this book was able to help you learn the basics of forex trading. The information you obtained from this book will serve you well in your desire to become a currency trader. By following the guidelines and instructions you found here, you'll have higher chances of reaping profits from the largest financial market in the world.

The next step is to continue analyzing the financial markets. Don't stop at currency-related information. Collect various types of data: as a forex trader, you'll never know which piece of information can lead to huge profits. In addition, you should keep on trading during your preferred market sessions.

Remember that the currencies are interconnected. A minor shift in the price of a currency pair can trigger price changes in other pairs. Thus, you should strive to be on top of the latest economic news and market developments. This way, you can obtain the knowledge you need to be a skilled forex trader.

Finally, if you enjoyed this book, please take the time to share your thoughts and post a review on Amazon. It'd be greatly appreciated!

Thank you and good luck!

www.ingramcontent.com/pod-product-compliance
Lightning Source LLC
Chambersburg PA
CBHW061157180526
45170CB00002B/838